# STEM IN SPORTS:
# ENGINEERING

# THE STEM IN SPORTS SERIES

**STEM in Sports: Science,** by Jim Gigliotti

**STEM in Sports: Technology,** by James Buckley, Jr.

**STEM in Sports: Engineering,** by Tim Newcomb

**STEM in Sports: Math,** by James Buckley Jr.

# STEM IN SPORTS:
# ENGINEERING

by Tim Newcomb

**Mason Crest**
450 Parkway Drive, Suite D
Broomall, PA 19008
www.masoncrest.com

@ 2015 by Mason Crest, an imprint of National Highlights, Inc.

Printed and bound in the United States of America.

Series ISBN: 978-1-4222-3230-9
Hardback ISBN:  978-1-4222-3231-6
EBook ISBN: 978-1-4222-8675-3

3 5 7 9 8 6 4

Produced by Shoreline Publishing Group LLC
Santa Barbara, California
Editorial Director: James Buckley Jr.
Designer: Patty Kelley
www.shorelinepublishing.com

Library of Congress Cataloging-in-Publication Data is on file with the publisher.

# CONTENTS

## KEY ICONS TO LOOK FOR:

 **Words to Understand:** These words with their easy-to-understand definitions will increase the reader's understanding of the text, while building vocabulary skills.

 **Sidebars:** This boxed material within the main text allows readers to build knowledge, gain insights, explore possibilities, and broaden their perspectives by weaving together additional information to provide realistic and holistic perspectives.

 **Research Projects:** Readers are pointed toward area of further inquiry connected to each chapter. Suggestions are provided for projects that encourage deeper research and analysis.

 **Text-Dependent Questions:** These questions send the reader back to the text for more careful attention to the evidence presented here.

 **Series Glossary of Key Terms:** This back-of-the-book glossary contains terminology used throughout this series. Words found here increase the reader's ability to read and comprehend higher-level books and articles in this field.

# INTRODUCTION

Sports build environments. From athletes to stadiums, sports culture shapes our world, and more than ever, engineers do the shaping. From the venues athletes play in to the cleats competitors wear, engineers provide sports' building blocks.

As the academic fields of STEM (Science, Technology, Engineering, and Math) continue to explore their creative side, we get to watch innovations on the world's largest sporting stages, from World Cups to Super Bowls to hometown gyms and fields. While athletes still perform the tasks we clamor to witness, engineers step in as an intricate behind-the-scenes pit crew. They pull data from sport and turn those bits of information into ideas for new equipment and training practices, along with fascinating new ways for fans to experience sports.

This volume of STEM in Sports explores engineering in sports. No part of the sports world will be untouched. Athletes now work with new data and equipment. Teams and leagues push the boundaries to thrill fans. The stadiums and fields of today balance the on-field needs of athletes with the desire to create a singular fan experience. And then there's the gear. Oh, the gear. It's a giant playground of new materials, forms, and functions.

The line between engineer and athlete can look big, but as the data-driven world of sports pushes forward, that gap collapses. That pushes STEM directly onto the field of play, on the feet and backs of athletes, and in every environment sports builds.

# CHAPTER 1

# ATHLETES

**E**VERY ATHLETE SEEKS THE SMALLEST OF EDGES. And to find those edges, more than ever before, they are turning to technology and engineering, both for the gear they use and the ways they train. Want to shave milliseconds off a sprint time? Turn to highly engineered cleats designed for immediate acceleration. Plan to train your brain to react quicker to in-game movements? You can find new data-driven training programs for that. Want to last a little longer in the game by protecting your body? Advances in equipment technology aim to take care of world-class athletes, all while improving on-field performance—and success.

**Before athletes reach the starting line, engineers get them ready to race.**

## Train the Brain

**P**UMPING IRON AND EXPANDING YOUR LUNGS WILL always play a critical role in sports performance, but athletes need to find new edges. For many, that kind of sharpness comes only from the brain.

The Mayo Clinic, an international leader in medicine, and USA Hockey, for example, use software developed to train Israel Air Force fighter pilots. It's all part of a **cognitive training** program geared toward on-ice performance. USA Hockey says the use of the IntelliGym program created by Applied Cognitive Engineering improves on-ice cognitive abilities by as much as 30 percent. A video-game-like interface—without storyboards or fantasy graphics, of course—helps players make all their moves more instinctive. Think of it as a workout tool for the mind.

Dr. Michael Stuart, the Mayo Clinic's Sports Medicine Center co-director, says that while training the brain remains a somewhat new idea, it is a part of sports that deserves more attention and research.

Stuart notes that a large segment of injuries, especially ones to the head, come from unanticipated hits in the open field or the open ice. "There is certainly merit to improving on-ice awareness and being able to anticipate plays before they happened," he tells *Sports Illustrated*. "Improving an athlete's

cognitive ability to see the game and understand it, through the help of programs such as IntelliGym, could prove helpful not only in skill development, but also injury prevention."

Nike, among others, wants athletes to improve all areas of their senses, including reaction time. Nike engineers created the SPARQ program, which pairs physical fitness with software programs to improve brain speed and function.

NFL wide receiver Greg Jennings says the program stimulates his mind and gets his

**USA Hockey reported that point-scoring rose 30 percent after its teams at all levels started using cognitive training exercises.**

competitive juices flowing. "It's not like a test," he says of the programs that use player interaction. "It's a competition you get hooked on, but you are actually improving your hand-eye coordination."

Nike has some hardware to go with it, too. The Vapor Strobe glasses remove visual senses during practice—the lenses were engineered to strobe on and off, removing an athlete's ability to see out of one or both lenses for bursts of time. Those bursts train the brain to react and perform with less information. Doing more with less in practice translates to an even greater reward when bombarded with sensory overload during the fast-paced movement of a professional sporting event.

"We give them less and less information, forcing the athletes to utilize what we give them more efficiently," says Dr. Allen Reichow, Nike's lead sensory performance researcher, "essentially doing stress training on the sensory system."

Playing with one eye? Vapor Strobe glasses train the brain to react to non-visual cues.

Seattle's Russell Wilson is one of hundreds of NFL pros who wear high-tech Nike jerseys and pants.

## More Than Just Looking Good

SURE, YOU CAN SLAP ON A FEW STRIPES AND ADD flashy colors and a city name across the front of a professional uniform and call it good. But engineers don't just work with machines, they work with fabric. And their skills are redefining what athletes wear.

Sports gear giants such as Nike and adidas use high-tech thermal and body mapping imagery to show where athletes sweat the most and when. They target those sports that need the most **ventilation** and cooling. In Nike's NFL uniforms, for example, designers used nine different materials, including fabrics that stretch four ways to tightly cling to the pads. Other parts of the jerseys include stretch-fit materials to eliminate grab points for the opposition or ventilation zones defined by lab testing.

During the 2014 World Cup in the heat of Brazil, Puma used brand-new taping and compression in uniform tops to strategically "micro-massage" specific areas of the skin during competition. The idea was to reduce muscle vibration and fatigue during the 90-minute games.

"By fusing athletic taping and compression, what we create is a system that enables faster energy supply to the muscles through the stimulation of the skin," says Jordi Beneyto Ferre, Puma innovation designer.

Adidas created a total kit (the European word for a player's uniform) at just 8.8 ounces (250 grams), a 40-percent reduction from what was previously available for World Cup teams. By designing with ultra-light polyester, adidas engineered in **moisture-wicking** materials, compression, and stretch materials.

Chile was one of six World Cup teams who turned to Puma's "micro-massage" uniforms to stay cool in Brazil.

# Body Parts

While we can all agree on the importance of protecting heads (they hold the brain, after all), other areas of the body deserve a little protection, too. Russell Athletic unveiled a new shoulder pad—the CarbonTek OS—for use in the 2014 NFL and Division I college football seasons made out of automobile-grade foams and aerospace-grade carbon fiber. The new pads create a larger protection area than ever before, but weigh 10 percent less. The overall weight is down to about four pounds (1.8 kg). A built-in compression vest holds a foam and carbon fiber exoskeleton that spreads out impact—63 percent less in the average force felt by the player.

NFL running back Mark Ingram, who tested the pads for Russell, says the CarbonTek felt more protective, and the snug fit gave him an even greater range of motion.

## Engineers Protect the Athlete

FINDING BETTER WAYS TO PROTECT ATHLETES HAS played a critical role in recent equipment advancements.

In football, for example, Riddell has stepped up its concussion-protection efforts with the Speedflex helmet. The new helmet, seen first in the 2014 season, works to dissipate force and keep impacts from rattling a player's head, instead transferring energy away from the brain as best it can.

The Speedflex helmet, shown here in a proposal drawing, could be standard in football in years to come.

Riddell engineers designed "flex" within the actual shell of the helmet, the facemask and where the facemask meets the helmet shell. That flex spreads the energy of a hit through the helmet, instead of transferring it to a player's head. Specifically engineered polyurethane foam and rubberized padding absorbs impact energy as well. The properties of the foam allow it to retain its shape and remain ready for the next impact. Coming in 2015, Riddell will step up its helmet tech even more, adding its

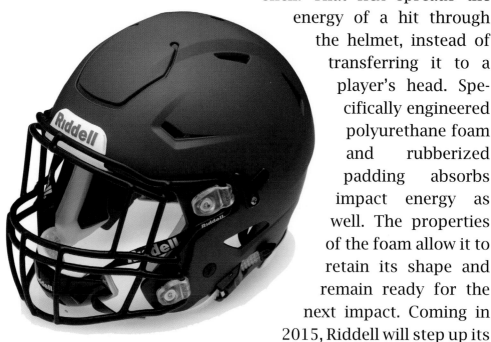

InSite Impact Response System in the Speed-flex to alert sideline trainers to the intensity of on-field impacts. The system will beam data from each hit to sideline monitors.

## TEXT-DEPENDENT QUESTIONS
*1. How can "training the brain" help an athlete on the field?*
*2. Why are tighter, better-fitting uniforms good for athletes?*
*3. How do new Riddell helmets spread force from blows to the head?*

## RESEARCH PROJECTS
*Find one of the "brain games" testing Web sites. Take some of the tests. Then try the "brain-ercise" they suggest and see if you can improve your results.*

# CHAPTER 2

# TEAMS & LEAGUES

**T**HE SUCCESS OF INDIVIDUAL ATHLETES LEADS TO personal triumph, but it also helps the teams and leagues for which the athletes compete. Having great athletes can not only help a team win, but it can help fill seats and attract outside interest from fans and sponsors. Leagues happily embrace success that leads to a more marketable venture. There are times, though, when it serves teams and leagues to do what they can to promote their sports as a whole. Engineering, especially in improving the fan experience of a sport, is playing a bigger and forward-thinking part in how teams and leagues present their products to the world.

**Without arena engineers, these hoops players would be outdoors on concrete instead of comfortably indoors!**

## Super Stadiums

THERE'S AN ART TO KEEPING FANS HAPPY. A successful on-field product certainly acts as one of the key features. Fans love a winner. But making sure that fans have fun win or lose is a big part of the game for pro sports.

Baseball teams have fun with the freedom to create. Little is set in stone when it comes to ballparks. In recent years, new parks have included fountains, slides, fish tanks, and even historic buildings. Whether an amusement park in Detroit or swimming pools in Arizona and Miami, it takes someone with design and engineering know-how to create that fun-filled, fan-friendly amenity.

Teams in the NBA and NHL don't have that same flexibility. Engineers have to get technical when they design venues hosting between 17,000 and 22,000 fans. With total seat capacity fairly set, the engineering creativity comes in figuring just how to place the people in the right places, all while still earning the team plenty of revenue. The balance of luxury seats—suites, club seats, and specialty "loge" seats that offer additional amenities—and average seats turns into a balance of revenue needs. That arrangement also defines how the building will look, the steepness of the seating areas, and the actual structural needs.

## WORDS TO UNDERSTAND

**façade:** The outside of a stadium or arena.

**glycol:** A fluid used in heating systems because it doesn't freeze when keeping its environment cool.

**GPS:** Global positioning system—technology that bounces a signal off satellites to pinpoint the exact location where the signal originated, such as the back of a player.

"The column spacing, roof trusses, building height, all those things are intimately driven by what happens in the [seating] bowl," says Jon Niemuth, director of sports for architect AECOM, the designer of the most NBA arenas in the league.

With the building's size and dimension defined by the space allowable (most arenas have to fit inside existing urban spaces), engineers still have room for fun. Soon, fans will be able to check out the 50-foot by 150-foot glass doors that will open a new Sacramento arena's **façade** designed by AECOM.

In the heat of Arizona, the Diamondbacks' home field sports a retractable roof to help keep fans and players cool.

NFL teams, with their huge stadiums holding 70,000-plus fans, don't design without the pinnacle of the sport in mind: the Super Bowl. To host a Super Bowl, a stadium must meet a long list of requirements. But those NFL-imposed rules don't always fit a team's local needs. Architects and engineers have found a way around that, along with a way to embrace it.

In San Francisco's new Levi's Stadium, which opened in August 2014, the needs of the local fan base matched with its hosting the Super Bowl in February 2016. Other parts required cleverness. The 1.85-million-square-foot stadium will fit the digital and wireless needs of the massive event with stadium-wide WiFi capability, mobile connectivity, 13,000 square feet of video boards, and mobile connection speeds that will impress Super Bowl fans. To accommodate the needs of this high-tech environment, engineers used the building itself. "Fiber optic raceways" were built within the stadium along with an unprecedented amount of server rooms and back-of-house space. The raceways will carry thousands of miles of cable for connections. Stadium designers from architect HNTB say what they did for the 49ers wouldn't be physically possible in even the NFL's largest venues because of the built-in engineering needed from the start.

As for fans in the seats, Levi's Stadium will

seat nearly 70,000. But for the Super Bowl, the NFL need even more seating—and plenty of space to party. Plazas on the northwest and southwest corners can convert into party spaces for fans during the Super Bowl. When you add in the space from two oversized party decks on either end of the end zone, you get more seating capacity without having to change the look of the venue. Engineering tricks turned Levi's Stadium from too small to host a Super Bowl to the perfect site.

Levi's Stadium was engineered for hi-tech Wi-Fi from the first moments of design.

## Taking the Game Outside

**H**OCKEY STARTED ON OUTDOOR ICE PONDS. NOW professionals play on ice in air-conditioned arenas. The NHL, though, enjoys a look to its roots. In recent years the Stadium Series has put a few regular-season games outside in the elements. Even though the games are outside in winter, Mother Nature needs help making sure the ice surface is cold and perfect for playing.

In fact, the NHL's outdoor games have been held in many climates, not just those with icy winter weather. Outdoor hockey in Los Angeles? No problem for winter engineers. For these outdoor games—such as the one held at Dodger Stadium between the Los Angeles

Hockey rink engineers went to work to put a full-size NHL rink on the field at Boston's Fenway Park in 2013.

Kings and the Anaheim Ducks—crews first level out a subfloor. On that, they placed 243 ice tray panels, each 28.5 feet long by 30 inches wide (8.7 m by 0.76 m) that rest on a **glycol** coolant system. In long tubes, more than 3,000 gallons of coolant loop under the ice to keep it at a perfect 22 degrees Fahrenheit (-5 Celsius). The NHL now has two mobile rink-refrigeration devices, each 53 feet (16.1 m) long and weighing 300 tons (304,000 kg). The glycol flows through the trucks and then under the ice in a constant, chilly stream.

Crews then spend about seven days misting 20,000 gallons (75,700 l) of tap water to create the two-inch (5 cm) surface. Inside the ice, 16 Eye on the Ice sensors alert crews to

any drop in temperature in the ice. To keep it all cozy, the NHL uses thermal blankets to keep the sun from melting away the newly frozen ice.

## Tracking Your Team

WANT TO KNOW EXACTLY HOW HARD YOUR EM-ployee is working? Monitor them. That may sound a bit creepy, but getting every possible competitive advantage for teams includes measuring player activity. The NFL has recently embraced this position, with several teams using data-tracking devices on players. The devices feed data to coach-

## Engineering Green

Engineers help teams improve on the field and create fan experiences, but they can also save teams money by going "green." In San Francisco's new Levi's Stadium, a tower on the west side, which includes luxury suites and the press box, also features solar panels on the 27,000-square-foot green roof. The panels will help the 49ers create energy, keeping their own costs down, and the green roof will cut energy usage.

Other stadiums are catching on, too. The Philadelphia Eagles' Lincoln Financial Field uses wind power to create energy. The Barclays Center in Brooklyn, home of the NBA's Nets, added a green roof that helps store solar energy and keep heat in the building. That venue not only made the arena more attractive, but the roof also helps reduce the noise from concerts held there.

ing staffs, providing specific player movements for fitness and tactical needs.

Using the Australian-made Catapult system, **GPS** technology strapped to the back of players can pinpoint player movements within six inches (15 cm), giving coaches information on acceleration, distance covered, speed, workout levels, hitting force, and every other imaginable piece of data.

With the data, teams can find weaknesses in a player's abilities in given situations. NFL coaches told Catapult that specific information—such as finding out which direction a wide receiver "explodes" better—changes the way they line up their players in formation.

Tom Myslinksi, the Jacksonville Jaguars' strength and conditioning coach, says the load of data helps him train players more efficiently.

## TEXT-DEPENDENT QUESTIONS

*1. What warm-weather site hosted an outdoor NHL game?*
*2. Why are indoor arenas more limited in their design than outdoor stadiums?*
*3. What NFL team plays in the new Levi's Stadium?*

## RESEARCH PROJECTS

*Research idea: You read here about teams using "green," sustainable design within their venues. Can you find other examples?*

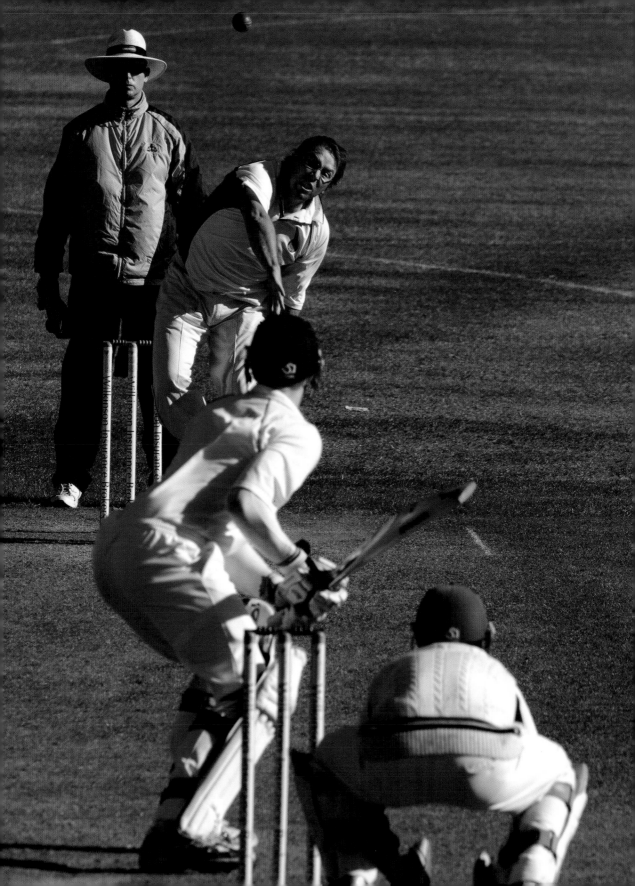

# CHAPTER 3

# ARENAS, FIELDS, AND FANS

WITHOUT A PLACE TO PLAY, THE ATHLETES we love to watch wouldn't have a platform on which perform. And without such places, we would have no way to witness their feats. In other words, you need stadiums—large, small, natural, or man-made. From massive football or soccer stadiums designed to enhance the crowd noise and comfort for 60,000-plus fans to small embellishments in natural bays for sailing, engineers step in to help create fan experiences. They also step up, making events possible by heating turf, designing new ways to watch events, and creating new environments to house our favorite sports.

**Around the world, from cricket pitches to NFL stadiums, engineers are seeking new ways to build places to play.**

## Managing Noise

**T**HE SUPER BOWL-CHAMPION SEATTLE SEAHAWKS gave an assist to their hometown fans, the ones that filled the 67,000-seat CenturyLink Field in downtown Seattle to cheer them on. The fans are known as the 12th Man. The huge volume of their cheering set a world record in 2013, but also helped create an NFL-leading number of opponents' false-start penalties.

Sure, Seattle needed crazed fans to make that noise, but the real assist should go to Jon Niemuth, the architect behind CenturyLink Field. How loud was it? In 2014, Seattle fans set a Guinness Record for loudest fan noise. The nearby University of Washington recorded small earthquakes when the fans went particularly nuts after massive plays.

Niemuth, though, planned it that way before Seattle opened its stadium in 2002. He designed the venue for noise. When Niemuth met with Seahawks owner Paul Allen before planning the design, Allen told him he wanted to create an atmosphere similar to a collegiate stadium..

The engineering behind the noise starts with creating a compact space. CenturyLink features the smallest **footprint** of any NFL stadium. But a tight footprint doesn't mean tiny space. CenturyLink's nearly 70,000 seats help put plenty of voices to work.

**WORDS TO UNDERSTAND**

**ETFE and PTFE:** Developed for use in space, these are high-tech plastics that are one percent the weight of glass with the ability to bear 400 times its own weight, while letting through 90 percent of sunlight that hits it.

**footprint:** In architecture, this means the ground area that a single building covers.

The high arches above the seats at CenturyLink direct fan noise back down to the field.

**hydronic:** A heating system that includes pipes placed under turf. The pipes run heated water and glycol through the pipes to warm the turf above.

**parabola:** A symmetrical curved path. In stadiums, a roof overhang can create a parabola by bouncing noise from below back down toward the field of play.

In the NFL, most non-dome stadiums are large, expansive bowls open wide to the sky. Sky is a noise killer, with the sound waves disappearing into the air. Not in Seattle, though, where 70 percent of all seats were covered to protect fans from the wet weather often seen in the Pacific Northwest. Niemuth designed the coverings with just right curves to bounce fan noise from the **parabola**-styled coverings directly toward the field.

## Put a Roof on It

SOMETIMES BAD WEATHER ENDS THE GAME. BASEBALL teams can't play in rain, for instance. Numerous rainouts make games an uncertainty for the ticket-buying public. Major tennis tournaments, such as the Grand Slams in Melbourne, Paris, London, and New York need the two-week tournament to stay on schedule to please both fans and television partners. And even sports that thrive in bad weather, such as the NFL, have a need to keep things dry, but not for the reason you think. With NFL stadiums now costing more than $1 billion to construct—but hosting fewer

This design drawing shows the new Arthur Ashe Stadium at the home of the U.S. Open of tennis.

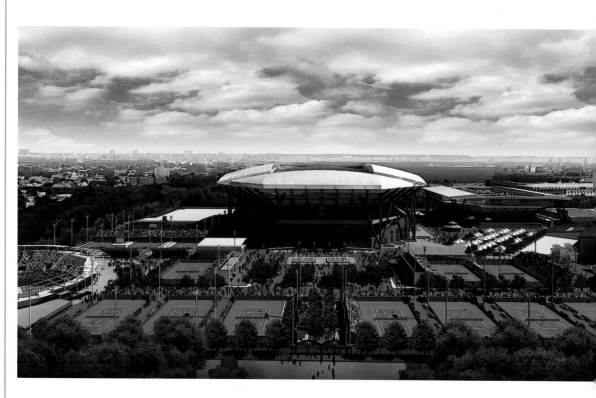

than a dozen games each year—the buildings' owners need other ways to make money. Concerts and conventions can't have the threat of rain ruining their events. When rain—or snow, for that matter—are a problem, the only choice is a stadium roof.

There are two ways to make a stadium roof: a permanent one or one that moves around. The latter are known as retractable roofs. The retractable roof option came alive in a big way in Toronto after Angus Robbie designed one of the first—and largest—retractable roofs of the day for SkyDome (now called Rogers Centre), which opened in 1989. That first major retractable design used steel wheels running on steel rails. The roof simply slid back. Since then, the engineering has changed.

Now we have roofs with steel or fabric and designs that pull into the center, retract into a fan, and more. The improvement in materials, such as **ETFE** plastic and **PTFE** fabric (something like Teflon), has given stadium engineers the options to branch out. No longer is the only way to cover the gaping hole a steel top rolling on steel wheels and rails.

Originally developed for the space industry, ETFE (ethylene tetrafluoroethylne) is a weather-resistant thermoplastic. Just one percent the weight of glass with the ability to bear 400 times its own weight, ETFE lets 90 percent of sunlight reach the turf.

That alone makes it a perfect choice for venues wanting the feeling of the outdoors, the light from sunshine when it comes, and none of the rain or snow.

Companies have even come up with ways to keep those roofs clean on their own, using organic substances that self-clean when UV light appears.

In New York City, where the Flushing Meadows Tennis Center hosts the U.S. Open every year, Arthur Ashe Stadium will soon have a retractable roof, an addition to help cope with the rain. But this simply wasn't possible with steel-only technology. The stadium is built on an old landfill site, so the stadium can't add heavy steel to its top with the unstable ground below. That's where the lightweight plastics and fabrics come in, giving designers a way to cover the stadium without adding unsupportable weight.

In Vancouver, British Columbia, where rain certainly threatens BC Place, stadium owners installed the world's largest cable-supported fabric roof, an engineering feet in and of itself. Using cables, the fabric roof—which cuts down on weight—retracts into the center of the building, neatly hiding away in the middle of the oversized center-hung scoreboard.

Atlanta has done something altogether different for its planned new NFL stadium, designing a roof that uses eight different

panels to create a new effect when opening. 360 Architecture's Bill Johnson says his design team started creating the proposed stadium with the roof to create an interesting piece of engineering that would drive the entire design and give Atlanta something truly different in the world of stadiums. "We wanted to do something that had never been done before," he says.

With that, the new Atlanta roof will start at the center, opening up with a pinpoint of light that continues to stream in and flow across the stadium floor as it opens. The

The tall towers above BC Place support a unique fabric-like roof that is strong but still lightweight.

# Indoor Grass?

One problem with indoor stadiums or retractable roofs: Sometimes that makes growing turf indoors difficult. The fix? Move the natural grass outside.

In Phoenix, where the roof stays closed so often due to the region's heat, having natural grass required a unique solution. The stadium has the first-ever retractable field, which pulls the entire field outside. Engineers devised a giant tray—roughly two acres—with 546 steel wheels atop 16 tracks on the stadium's floor. The tray (at bottom in the picture) can't

just hold dirt and grass. The entire 39-inch (99-cm) deep tray includes drainage and irrigation systems and moves through a 200-foot (61-m) wide opening in the bottom of the stadium. The tray takes about an hour and a quarter to roll outside and soak in the Phoenix sun.

When engineers couldn't bring the sun in, they found a way to bring the grass to the sun.

eight-panel roof looks almost like a series of wedges rotating as they move. In reality, each panel moves in a straight line and eventually exposes 110,000 square feet of space over the playing surface, almost like falcon wings opening up the light. Johnson says he opted for the super lightweight ETFE material with more benefits than just toughness and weight: transparency. Using an engineered system, the Falcons will be able to control the product to change how much—or how little—light they want to let in.

Sometimes, though, spending the money on a roof that moves around just doesn't make sense. Some climates—or budgets, for that matter—call for a roof always closed. The ETFE material does the job. In Minneapolis, the Vikings' new NFL stadium will feature a roof that will let the natural light, but not the natural snow, enter the stadium. The ETFE lets in so much light that Forsyth Barr Stadium in New Zealand became the first permanently covered stadium in the world to grow an all-natural turf field. The 30,000-seat venue opened in 2011 with enough natural light to keep the grass growing, while also keeping the fans protected from the outside.

## Heating Up

FREEZING TEMPERATURES AFFECT MORE THAN JUST fans and players. The stadiums get plenty chilly, too, especially the playing surfaces. NFL stadiums throughout the North use heating systems underneath their fields. Such systems keep both natural-grass surfaces and synthetic fields from freezing.

From the obvious cold-weather locations of Denver and Green Bay straight to the Northeast, engineers have devised heating systems that keep grass and the concrete aprons around the field warm enough to ensure a safe playing surface. Nearly a dozen NFL groundskeepers fire up **hydronic** heating systems buried up to a foot (0.3 m) under the turf. By pumping warm chemicals through the pipe system, groundskeepers can keep the soil temperatures above freezing, even in the toughest of winters. The systems aren't designed to melt snow as it falls, but they can keep the fields from feeling like concrete.

In Green Bay, for example, grounds crews will run its glycol and water mixture heated in an on-site boiler through the piping under the turf at 38 degrees F (3.3 C). That temperature is plenty warm to keep Lambeau's famed "frozen tundra" from actually freezing and becoming dangerous for players. But it also remains cool enough to let the grass toughen up and offer the feeling of cold-weather football.

Underground heating systems make sure that the players are not performing on frozen grass in Green Bay.

In other places, though, such as Philadelphia, Baltimore and Denver, crews fire up to 20 miles (32 km) of plastic tubing about 10 inches (25 cm) below the turf. The pipes are spaced about nine inches apart to get grass and turf temperature all the way into the 50s F (10 C).

The NFL isn't the only place to pull off heating feats. MLB stadiums have similar systems. In Minneapolis, to coax grass to grow in time for the start of the season in early April, a system tricks the grass into thinking spring has come, even if snow still falls. The MLB stadiums in Seattle, Denver, and New York's Citi Field also have systems that help warm the turf through forced-air, electric coils or hydronic processes. KC Stadium in Hillsborough, England, home of the Premier League's Hull City club, also has turf-heating piping, as does Emirates Stadium in London, home to Arsenal.

Bitter cold may get to the human element, but engineers have ensured the stadiums don't let the cold bother them one bit.

## Going Natural

WATCHING SPORTS DOESN'T ALWAYS NEED A stadium or grass. Some sports cover much more ground!

The America's Cup is a sailing competition that is one of the oldest sporting events in the world, having started way back in 1851. During the 2013 event, 12-story tall, carbon fiber, fixed-wing sailboats zipped in tight spaces of picturesque San Francisco Bay. Organizers used the natural shoreline for seating and the Golden Gate Bridge, Alcatraz, and more as the backdrop. But even in the outdoors, high-tech treatments are needed.

The finely tuned multi-million-dollar boats were engineered to the smallest of margins, with testing and tweaking done only with high-tech data. On board, oceans of data-tracking devices helped inform teams of every possible race condition and boat performance metric. But getting the fans involved was challenging, too. America's Cup organizers built two grandstands on San Francisco piers, offering live commentary, stores, exhibits, and bleachers. The Pier 27 site located along the busy Embarcadero added a concert stage and set up the high-tech broadcast on a giant screen, requiring engineers not only to create the fastest America's Cup boats we'd ever seen, but also to make

Tens of millions of dollars went into the design of America's Cup sailboats.

something of a pop-up stadium in San Francisco's natural environment.

Each year a similar marvel occurs when Tour de France organizers handle the onslaught of 21 racing stages across multiple countries. (In 2014, the race started in England before moving to France and dipping into Spain and Belgium.) And while you won't see stadium-style seating all that often during Le Tour, expect plenty of high-tech work. Start with about 4,000 people traveling along with the riders. The worldwide popularity of the event requires 50 technicians to set up

This drawing shows the buildings and grandstands that were built to give fans a way to watch the 2013 America's Cup.

500 high-flow media cable lines, five Wi-Fi networks, 87 mobile relays, and more than 9 miles (15 km) of cable at every stage along the 1,860-plus-mile (3,000-km-plus) course.

Everywhere sports occurs and people gather to watch, engineers must step in and provide the know-how to make it happen. And make it so we can watch.

## Re-Engineering Tradition

Daytona International Speedway opened in 1959. But by 2016 the old track will have a completely different form. In a first-ever event, Daytona is turning its antiquated grandstand into a racing stadium, rebuilding one of the largest stadium venues in the world. More than 40 million pounds (18.2

Here's a view of Daytona in 2014; it won't look like this after a massive renovation is completed.

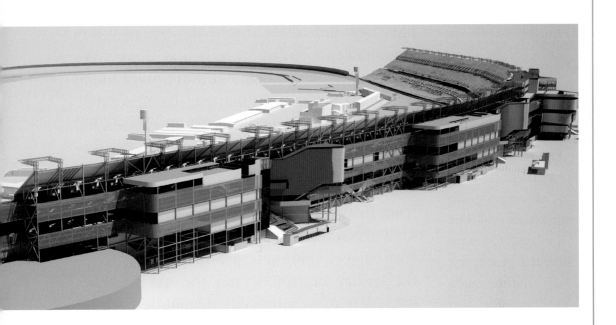

million kg) of steel will turn the nearly one-mile (1.6 km) front stretch grandstand that seats about 100,000 into something completely different than what fans have long known.

The old track looked pretty low-tech before the $400-million "Daytona Rising" plan to recreate the stadium started taking shape in late 2013. Daytona had simple grandstand-style seats that required fans to walk as much as 70 feet (21 m) from the ground to the top of the stands. Engineers devised a way to change all that, completely redoing the stands to raise the stadium to 146 feet (44.5 m) tall, adding in concourses and entries into the seats from behind (similar to a typical stadium). The shorter walks to seats

This design drawing shows some of the features that will be added to the "new" Daytona.

plus new amenities that make the race day experience more fan-friendly.

Redoing an existing stadium proves much tougher than simply starting from scratch. Construction crews need to insert 40,000 individual pieces of steel into an existing structure, completely changing the way the stands work. To make it happen, engineers from firms across the country work together digitally in real-time to ensure the right plans and correct materials are in place. Without the luxury of ripping out the old stadium, engineers must surgically dismantle parts of the old steel in order to install the new grand-

The racing action at Daytona calls on engineering muscle as well, but fans will focus on how the new track means more comfort and better views.

stands, concourse, concessions, restrooms, and elevators. And how big is the site? Daytona is so large that engineers have to take into account the 7-inch (17.7 cm) curvature of the earth over the course of the nearly one-mile-long (1.6 km) stadium.

## TEXT-DEPENDENT QUESTIONS

*1. How do cold-weather stadiums keep the grass from freezing?*
*2. Why was building seating for the America's Cup so challenging?*
*3. How does the Seattle Seahawks' stadium help the team's fans be so loud?*

## RESEARCH PROJECTS

*Look at images of some of the stadiums mentioned here, then look at older venues such as Fenway Park, Lambeau Field, or Wrigley Field. How do they look different? List the differences in design and materials.*

# CHAPTER 4

# GEAR

**Thanks to new materials, racing bikes are stronger—but lighter—than ever.**

THE IDEAS THAT ENGINEERS HAVE COME UP WITH to revolutionize the sports gear industry weren't even figments of their imaginations in earlier days. Super-engineered yarn as the latest and greatest way to create a shoe? Using a 3-D printer to research how a sprinter moves? Bulletproof carbon fiber to build a Tour de France bicycle? Dyes that change eye colors to help extreme sport athletes? The list reads like an engineer's dream, a list that doesn't have an end and will only grow with "Ah ha!" moments of discovery. Before athletes can compete, they need to gear up. And they need engineers to help them do that with style and substance.

## A Long Yarn

**N**IKE, THE OREGON-BASED SHOE-MAKING LEADER, did something unexpected when it started creating the shoe material of the future: The company engineered yarn.

Called **Flyknit**, Nike took the stretchy properties and comfort of that sock-like product and created ways to harden it into shoes for tracks and gyms. Flyknit debuted in 2012 in a running shoe, but now is part of soccer, football, and basketball models, too. The one-piece upper parts of the shoes are made from a single strand of the Flyknit yarn. This gets rid of seams that add weight and rub against feet. Nike micro-engineered properties into this yarn so that it worked with other parts of the shoe to create many options for designers: waterproof coatings, Kevlar bands for strength, a wide array of colors, and more.

What started in running, though, really took off when other sports chimed in on the fun. Of the two Flyknit boots (which is what the rest of the world calls soccer cleats), one is built for speed and includes an especially thin knit, just three layers with the right amount of rigidity. The other soccer boot, though, is about controlling the ball, so Nike engineers added a 3-D texture to the Flyknit. This increases the friction between cleat and ball, improving player control.

Whether the Kobe Bryant signature bas-

## WORDS TO UNDERSTAND

**carbon fiber:** A material woven of carbon atoms that offers a wide range of high-strength and high-flexibility properties.

**Flyknit:** Nike's micro-engineered yarn that has static properties to support its shoes.

**prototype:** a model of a future product made to test design and engineering issues.

**wavelengths:** The measurements used to define different colors of light. The energy of light moves in waves; the distance between the waves is the wavelength.

ketball shoe or a soccer cleat, Nike has different styles of cables—Kevlar-like Flywire and Brio—that can weave directly into the Flyknit to add strength exactly where the foot needs it and nowhere else, reducing overall weight and bulk.

## Shoe Printers?

GETTING A NEW SHOE TO MARKET INCLUDES YEARS of research and development. All along the process, prototype shoes are designed to help perfect each product. They used to be made overseas after being designed on a computer. Now, 3-D printing has revolutionized the development process for shoe manufacturers. With a 3-D printer, they can make numerous **prototype** designs—with

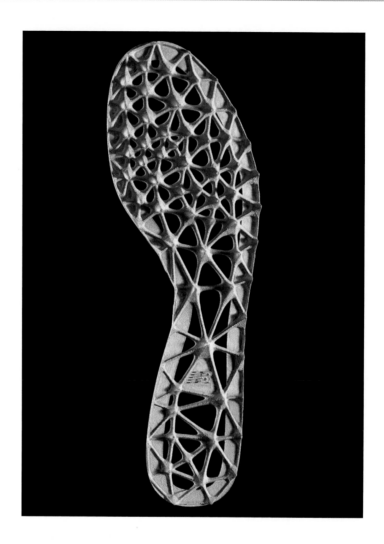

New Balance created this spike pattern for distance runner Jack Bolas using 3-D printer tech.

tweaks made on the spot—in a single testing session.

The molds the printer makes mean more options and choices for designers. It also helps make customized shoes, opening up new areas of business.

At New Balance, for example, designers created customized track spike plates for the company's elite athletes. They made shoes for each athlete based on data collected from the athlete's foot. After testing, they could make new models instantly, saving lots of time and thousands of dollars.

Nike, which employs a similar model, used its process to help design new football cleats, created for position-specific movements. Athletes wearing Nike's 3-D printed cleat set the fastest 40-yard-dash times at the NFL's Scouting Combine, an event designed to measure the abilities of incoming rookies. Designed specifically for immediate acceleration, Nike 3-D printing gave athletes a new way to win.

## Biking on Air?

TWENTY-THREE OUNCES. 652 GRAMS. ENGINEERS at Cervelo, a high-end bicycle manufacturer, created a carbon-fiber bicycle frame weighing a featherweight 23 ounces. That's lighter than the full water bottle you carry with you on the ride and the lightest bike on the market by the time the 2014 Tour de France rolled around.

This new generation of **carbon fiber**, with some fiber layers 10 times as stiff as others, has embraced the flow of fiber, with each of the 500 layers of carbon on Cervelo's Rca bikes designed individually. Cervelo uses five different versions of fiber, some mixed with Kevlar to optimize strength and flexibility.

The highest-strength fibers are in the down tube and the seat tube. Small additions, such as adding nickel coating to carbon fiber, can increase strength on high-stress points.

When riders add in their wheels and the extras pros require, the finished product comes to as little as 10 pounds (4.5 kg), a highly engineered fine-tuning of carbon fiber and weight. Weights have gone so low that international cycling organizers make each bike reach a minimum weight for races to make sure of an evenly-matched event. Cyclists sometimes have to *add* weight!

## Warm Like a Goose

Goose down is one of the best natural warming materials. But while natural goose feathers keep us warmer than anything man has made to date, they don't do so well when they get wet and flatten out.

The North Face improved the goose, creating the ThermoBall coat, a mix of tiny insulation balls that do what down does, but withstand water. They "stand up," or stay fluffy even when wet. That means that the coat does the same thing with air that real goose down does—bouncing warm air toward the body, instead of away from it. The end result gives The North Face a lightweight—11 ounces (312 g)—cold-weather coat nearly the same as down. Consider actual down goosed.

## Going Downhill . . . Fast!

**N**OT TO BE OUTDONE BY THE RIDERS ON THE TOUR de France, bobsledders in the Olympics embrace carbon fiber, too. Team USA turned to auto manufacturer BMW to create the bobsled used during the 2014 Winter Olympics in Russia.

BMW took sleds into its California-based DesignWorksUSA research facility and fine-tuned the perfect sled. That was more than just a few tweaks, however. The process included a complete overhaul of the sled, all while embracing carbon fiber in an entirely new way.

**Auto racing engineering helped US bobsledders earn Olympic medals.**

During the testing process, BMW placed athletes in sleds to test aerodynamics in a wind tunnel, especially in the twisting and turning motions a sled makes on the ice.

In the end, BMW and Team USA created a narrower sled that whittled away excess weight. It must have worked pretty well: U.S. sleds brought home four medals from the Games, including America's first in the four-man event since 1952!

## Tennis Rockets?

TEAM U.S.A. BROUGHT IN BMW FOR ITS BOBSLEDS. Wilson Tennis went with missile-tracking technology to upgrade its latest line of rackets.

Using the same radar testing as missile-tracking gear, Wilson measured the way a tennis ball reacted to the racket strings. Spin is a key factor in tennis. Engineers needed a real-time way to measure how strings and racket worked together to spin the ball. John Lyons, global product director for Wilson Racquet Sports, told *Sports Illustrated* that his company's live-tracking system measures flight, speed, rotation, and height over the net.

A new arrangement of strings on this Wilson tennis racket will give the player more control of the spin of the ball.

The research showed Wilson that it was time to change how racket strings are arranged. The company went through 38 different patterns. But to create a way for the best pattern to fit the racket meant re-engineering the racket, too. Wilson used up to 10 different layers of carbon fiber, put on in different angles, to create the Wilson Spin Effect racket head that keeps the ball on the strings for one valuable extra millisecond. The end result was a ball with an additional 200 RPMs (revolutions, or spins, per minute). That's bad news for anyone facing this powerful new athletic tool.

## Eyes on the Prize

YOUR EYES BRING IN COUNTLESS WAVELENGTHS OF light. But during a high-speed athletic performance all those wavelengths drown out some of the most important data—the flow of the current in the ocean, the reach of a branch on a downhill mountain biking trail, or the change in the asphalt while road biking, for example.

Oakley has engineered help, creating more than 70 different lens tints in glasses. Athletes can choose which wavelengths they see to help their performance.

As Scott Betty, Oakley's global director of optics, says, you don't play baseball in soccer cleats, so you shouldn't perform outside in

British cyclist Mark Cavendish benefits from Oakley lens technology during long road races.

the wrong set of eyewear. Oakley's optic science blends the right colors and wavelengths for the correct environments.

For example, road runners or bikers wear a gray tint. This helps details in the black asphalt roads pop out. Mountain trail runners and bikers wear lenses that open up red, yellow, and orange. This helps them see details of the muddy, rocky soil more clearly and safely. Golfers can see shades of green better, while fishermen can get a more accurate view beneath the water's surface more easily . . . if they're wearing the right lenses.

To block the bad light and welcome the good light, Oakley mixes up to 20 different dyes or basic pigments into polycarbonate lenses, making them in a special way that cuts glare. That all keeps athletes looking right . . . in more ways than one.

Engineers are working on every part of athletes' bodies, from their feet to their eyes, in an effort to create ways to win.

## TEXT-DEPENDENT QUESTIONS

*1. What new technology is changing the way that shoes are designed?*
*2. What industry helped the U.S. win bobsled gold?*
*3. Why do different colored lenses help athletes succeed?*

## RESEARCH PROJECTS

*Research idea: Gear has turned increasingly high-tech, with engineers exploring new materials. Pick a piece of sports equipment and explain why using new materials would improve it.*

# WINNING . . . AND THE FUTURE

# CHAPTER 5

In decades past—especially the ones in your history books—the thought of engineers playing a vital role in sports, let alone recreational and professional sports, was laughable. Now engineering is as much a part of sports as training, coaching, and athletes. But have engineering advances been a positive change for the direction of sports? It's a debate that is ongoing in front offices and sports equipment makers everywhere.

With the rate of change still speeding along, though, don't expect to see athletes, coaches, trainers, owners, officials, equipment manufacturers, and others sit back and let others beat them. They don't want their opponents to find that next millisecond faster time, or create the athlete-safety device or fan-welcoming stadium idea that will make millions. In fact, the rate of change in the future may fly past what we've already seen.

Take stadiums, for example. In the 1960s and 1970s, teams and leagues built concrete monstrosities: giant, boring bowls that could house

#12 LINCOLN - .314

91 MPH

Forward-thinking engineers are looking at new ways to get fans close to the action. This mockup shows fans looking through glass walls at game action. From the field, the walls show ads or colors.

everything from football to baseball to giant conventions. There was little in the way of fan amenities or entertaining touches. That all changed with the advent of sport-specific architecture—stadiums and arenas built just for each sport. That trend continues to evolve.

The stadiums of the future will only get more diverse and interconnected between the data and technology of the players and the interest of the fans. The architectural firm Populous—the designer of the most baseball stadiums in Major League Baseball—envisions stadiums that mesh with cities, almost like storefronts on the outside that open to a ballpark field inside. Their vision includes exteriors that can double as retail or office space, and then morph into specialized suites. City parks will connect to the fields for year-round use. And don't forget all the technology.

Maybe we'll see suites that have smart-boards displaying real-time statistics, graphics, and data from the game. Or, if hard-hitting football is your thing, the stadiums of the future might have seats that vibrate at an intensity that exactly matches a play on the field. Imagine setting your seat to mimic the experience of your favorite team's quarterback, rattling your body at the same level as the hit he just took on the field. Of course, these types of possibilities beg the question: Will we create too many experiences, or will we drown in data, and lose the simple thrill of the games?

No matter how we answer that question now, we know the future of sports hasn't yet been fully defined. It constantly innovates, thanks to engineers creating a new way to look at sports, athletes, stadiums, and gear. Using tools like never before, sport engineers continue to build.

# FURTHER RESOURCES

## Books
### Football Stadiums
By Lew Freedman
Firefly Books, 2013
A wide-ranging guide to pro and college stadiums.

### The Kids' Guide to Sports Design and Engineering
By Thomas Anderson
SI for Kids Guides, 2014
(Note: The title says "kids" but this book includes some high-tech info for all readers.)

### Sports Technology
By Stewart Ross
New Apple Media, 2012

## Web Sites
### populous.com
Click through the many examples of groundbreaking sports arena and stadium design at this site, home of the worldwide architectural firm.

### popularmechanics.com/outdoors/sports/
*Popular Mechanics*, one of the world's best magazines for hands-on science, has a section of its site devoted to sports technology and engineering.

# SERIES GLOSSARY: WORDS TO UNDERSTAND

**aerodynamic** The science of how air moves and how objects move through it

**applications** In this case, ways of using information in a specific way to find answers

**carbon fiber** A material woven of carbon atoms that offers a wide range of high-strength and high-flexibility properties

**cognitive training** Software and hardware that trains the brain and the body's senses

**fluid dynamics** The science of how air or liquid moves over a surface

**GPS: Global positioning system** Technology that bounces a signal off satellites to pinpoint the exact location of where the signal originated from

**logistics** The science of organizing large numbers of people, materials, or events

**parabola** A symmetrical curved path. In stadiums, a roof overhang can create a parabola by bouncing noise from below back down toward the field of play.

**prosthetics** Devices that replace a missing human limb

**prototype** A model of a future product made to test design and engineering issues

**rehabilitation** The process of returning to full physical ability through exercise

**velocity** Measurement of the speed of an object

**ventilation** The easy movement of air around or within a body or a system

# INDEX

## Photo Credits

## About the Author

**Tim Newcomb** is a freelance journalist based in the Pacific Northwest. He covers stadiums, design, and gear for *Sports Illustrated,* and sports and infrastructure for *Popular Mechanics.* His work has also appeared in *Time, Popular Science, Wired, Fast Company, Dwell, Stadia* and a variety of publications across the world. Follow him on Twitter at @tdnewcomb.